D1609276

FABRIC COLLAGE

FABRIC
COLLAGE

Contemporary
Stitchery
and Appliqué

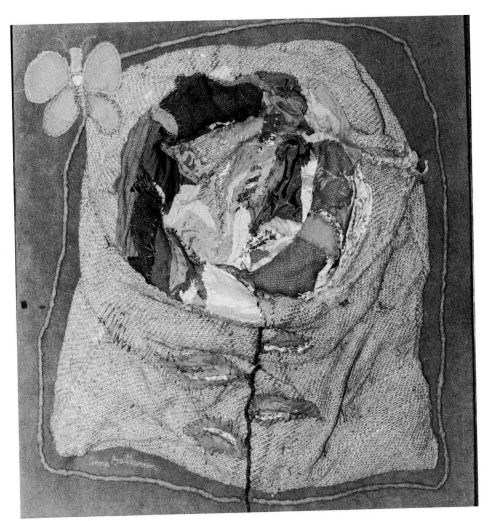

Anna Ballarian
Professor of Art,
San Jose State University

Davis Publications, Inc.
Worcester, Massachusetts

Copyright 1976
Davis Publications, Inc.
Worcester, Massachusetts, U.S.A.

Printed in the United States of America
Library of Congress Catalog Card
    Number: 76-29553
ISBN: 0-87192-089-1

Printing: Davis Press, Inc.
Binding: A. Horowitz and Son
Type: Optima by Davis Press, Inc.
Graphic Design: Penny Darras and Diane
    Nelson, Thumbnail Associates
Consulting Editors: George F. Horn and
    Sarita R. Rainey

Cover illustration:
Delicate Bouquet by the author.

Page one:
Still Life by Nancy Freeman.

Title page:
*Use of Litter Bag Will Help Keep Our
Country Beautiful.* The author.

10 9 8 7 6 5 4 3 2 1

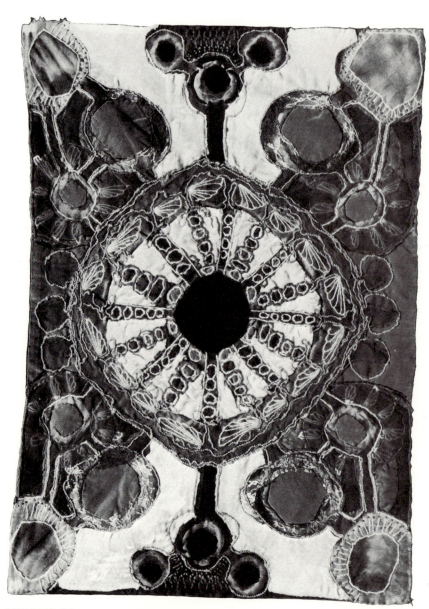

Middle Pink by Joanne Miller Johnson is a
joyful expression. The composition is a
mirrored reflection of circular forms in
shades of pink.

Contents

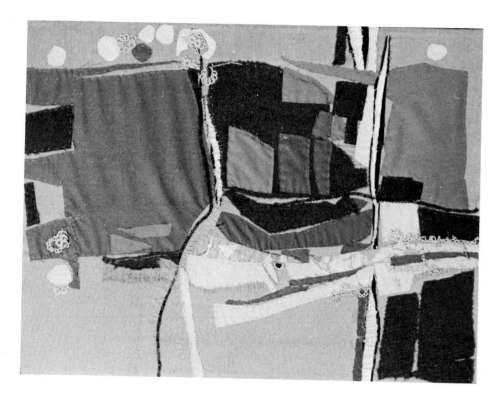

A seamstress' discards, with slight alterations in the shapes, forms *Green Landscape* by the author. Tatted lace is used for an irregular texture.

Aerial Garden. Joanne Miller Johnson illustrates how an idea evolved through direct experimentation with fabrics and threads.

The term collage is a picture or ornamental design composed of paper, fabric, fiber, photographs or other similar materials. Fabric collage is a process of appliquéing materials together by sewing or gluing. Stitching is used to decorate or reinforce the materials. Most any embroidery stitch or any material is acceptable.

Fabric collage stitchery is simply the art of attaching pieces of material arranged in some aesthetic relationship on a background to form a design. The new developments in fabrics can inspire a wide range of experiments. Ideas can be flat, projecting from surfaces or hang beyond the frame. It is the perfect medium for a person interested in creating something personal and original to enhance one's environment or personal dress. The instantaneous results and the ability to communicate ideas with fabrics and threads can give pleasure to the inexperienced adult or child or the serious artist.

The personal tactile associations, the actual handling of the cloth and thread, the quality of the cloth and threads, invites abstract ideas that reflect the thinking of a painting, sculpture or any other form of art. But true originality is achieved by applying basic properties of materials and techniques to fabrics and threads that are sympathetic in an innovative way.

Introduction

Sources of design, methods of developing an idea, and other technical information will be discussed. Constant awareness of visual experiences will be emphasized for new approaches for creative results. Although one may not become an accomplished artist, an appreciation for the effort that is involved in creating any work of art can be developed.

Back view of L.K.M. jacket.

L.K.M. jacket. Lucille Margosian exhibits the unique appliqué with dress labels on the interior of the jacket, a pleasing contrast to the textured exterior.

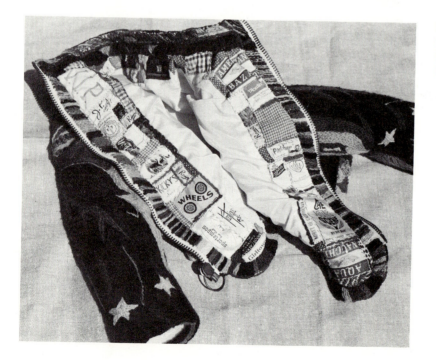

1

Cultural Influences

St. George's Cope. Courtesy of the
Church of St. Matthew in San Mateo,
California.

Collage, as we know it, began with the innovations of Braque and Picasso. The term, itself, has become an accepted part of the art vocabulary. Fabric collage stitchery developed out of the early appearance of collage as a folk art. Centuries ago, folk art was considered only as a pastime and not taken too seriously.

To ornament the environment by painting, drawing or placing designs on walls and on the body has always been natural to humans. From primitive cultures to the present time, folk art has also been popular. Today, with the advance of technological processes of printing, weaving and dyeing, the production of colorful and textured designs on fabrics is possible. This leads to fresh insights in recognizing the versatility of fabrics for the newer concept of collage in pictures, sculptural constructions and functional art objects.

Embroidery is used in collage to embellish the fragments of cloth and to provide a relief effect. In the seventeenth century, English stump work mingled embroidery with gluing in three-dimensional ways, accomplished by padding the embroidery to attain a kind of realism. In earlier times, glues were often home-made and if they did not stick, pictures were then stitched together. But with the reliability of adhesives and the variety of threads on the market today, craftspeople have enthusiastically produced fabric collage with gluing and stitching, for both practical and expressive effects.

The easy communication and transportation of today promotes an intermingling of cultural ideas. This influence is greatly felt in designs and techniques of contemporary fabric collage stitchery. Traditionally, many of these decorated fabrics were results of religious experiences, superstitious beliefs, everyday needs, or merely designs for enrichment to satisfy the eye. It is through our rich heritage of past generations that the modern designer can meet the challenge of our continually changing culture.

A search into our own ancestry can be one worthwhile source for re-establishing personal identity in our multi-ethnic society. It stimulates excitement to become involved in creating new designs.

Students enjoy the opportunity to research their own cultural background. It is a quick way to become involved in commencing a creative

The delicate spidery-like quality of Armenian lace makes this handwork different from that of another culture. Photograph by George Gananian.

venture. As a result, many family treasures can be unearthed and shared in a classroom situation.

In each period of art history particular techniques and expressions were emphasized. This was evident in the exquisite craftsmanship of patterned fabric in appliqué and embroidery of eastern countries, as for example, Persia. Persians, encouraged and stimulated by the conquering Mohammedans, showed a high degree of excellence in design. No representational forms were permitted by the prophet Mohammed. But the Persians rare selective interpretation of conventionalizing natural form shows a rhythmic arrangement of pattern and color in combining fabrics and stitches. Mosaic-like designs cut from handwoven fabrics are held together by outlined cord sewn down in some of the work. The Persian Resht possesses it's own characteristics being composed of felted woolen cloth with strong outlines.

Persian Resht.

Our Mother Moist Earth, 2½' x 4', Huichol
Indian yarn painting by Jose Bénitez Sanchez. Courtesy of Juan Negrin, photograph by Lloyd Patrick Baker.

Emergence Out of Darkness, Huichol Indian yarn painting by Juan Rios Martinez.
Property of George H. Howell, photo-
graphy by John Knaggs.

Fantasy birds are the source of idea in this San Blas mola. Ideas grew out of traditional body painting, intended to ward off evil spirits.

The spontaneous design approach as observed in the extraordinary Huichol Indian yarn painting can also serve as an inspiration to the fabric collage stitchery artist. Brilliant colored yarns are wound round and round into pictures impressed in an adhesive mixture of beeswax, paraffin and rosin spread on a thin plywood surface.

Most Huichol artists do not make a preliminary sketch. Ideas intuitively develop from the imagination inspired from their cultural heritage. Designs are expressions of sacred experiences symbolic of nature — the sun, moon and water. Much of the Huichol's expressions are guided by his religious way of life.

The imaginative and colorful fabric appliqué with the elaborate stitchery by the Indian women of the San Blas Islands, a group of small islands off the eastern shores of Panama, has been another one of the early influences for the contemporary fabric collage stitchery artist. The technique is called reverse appliqué. This creative stitched collage is made into blouses called molas, worn as ceremonial dress. The design ideas originate from environmental sources, bible stories and advertisements. They are wholly abstract.

In primitive civilizations and peasant cultures, worn out clothing was repaired with pieces of fabric scraps, sometimes enriched with stitches. The cut out shapes were hemmed down and often were attached to decorate articles. Distinguishing costume characteristics of Bedouin tribes, for instance, show a series of patches of cloth appliquéd to the original garment. Some backgrounds show rich embroidery that gives them color and beauty.

Church vestments with applied fabric can be found in early French and English Medieval churches. The edges of the fabric pieces were outlined with a cord or silk stitched down to clean up the edges. Applied fabric has historically been used as a less costly substitute for covering surfaces with solid embroidery.

In Palestine and Greece, for instance, designs were copied from other regions, reworked and reinterpreted to suit the individual embroiderer's application. Because of this individual interpretation, it is very often difficult to identify the origin of every motif.

Today, Egyptians are making fabric patchwork that is undoubtedly a development of the very art practised in Cleopatra's time. They use the appliquéd work for cushions, panels for screens and wall hangings. Generally, loosely woven cotton and a firm coarse linen are used in their construction. The cottons are dyed in plain bright colors and appliquéd on

Egyptian appliqué exemplifies some of the subjects taken from daily life.

natural colored backgrounds. The patchwork designs are typically Egyptian and many pieces show designs taken from tombs and temples.

It was in pioneer America that the art of the utilitarian quilt reached heights of perfection. Contemporary fabric collage draws heavily in this art form for design sources and ideas. As a craft form it flourished in rural areas in which new cloth was scarce. Every scrap of used cloth was reshaped into patterns and stitched together for bedding to protect them from the cold winters. The quilting bee was part of their social life.

Because of their hardships the sturdy pioneer quiltmakers reflected their feelings and thoughts in their quilt designs. Titles, such as "Tippecanoe", "Lincoln's Platform" and "Democrat Rose" show that women, as well as men, had an interest in politics.

Important events were recorded in quilts. The commemorative quilt, given to the Victoria and Albert Museum in 1961, was of especially manufactured commemorative textile prints, dating from the end of the 18th century, in fabric patchwork. Many designs, such as the log cabin quilt, popular in the 19th century, were so called because of the square blocks. The patches, surrounded by strips of material representing logs, were overlapped at the corners in much the same fashion as the log cabins were built. All odds and ends of wool, cotton and silk were used.

A detailed section of an early American crazy quilt, made of bits and pieces of old clothing, outlined with various stitches.

Designs were handed down from one generation to the next. Many museums have prized quilt collections. Among the better know collections are those at the Shelburne Museum in Vermont, the Smithsonian Museum in Washington, D.C. and in the Victoria and Albert Museum in London. The revival of interest today shows that even though traditional techniques are used, twentieth-century methods and materials encourage new directions in design.

Crazy quilt, courtesy of George Numan. Early American example shows fabrics intricately joined together with traditional embroidery.

2

Inspiration for Design Ideas

Series of sketches of the same subject
could develop into interesting design
ideas.

Photograph of bare branches against sky.

Photograph of dry stream bed with mud cracks and ripples. Photograph by Robert Ishi.

The world is full of visual and tactile experiences. Observing the bare dark branches of a tree against the light sky can be easily interpreted in fabrics. Enjoying pattern in a dry stream bed with mud cracks and ripples can be expressed with couched threads. Seeing colors and shapes reflected in a pool are an invitation to respond with colored fabrics. Observation of these contrasting surfaces and the effect of light directed on them creates a conscious awareness to design. Light and shade give definition to shape.

Interest to create depends upon the curiosity to see design in everything surrounding us from the largest to the smallest, the ocean waves to a grain of sand. To keep alive this curiosity, it is worthwhile to build up a ready reference file of photographs and sketches of things observed. These experiences can later be drawn upon for creative work.

Bark of tree.

The kind of response to a particular experience will vary according to the level of interest and background of a person. While some people may seem to have a natural gift for design, others may need guidance. No matter what the level of experience, basic knowledge of techniques is needed to gain confidence.

Selecting a Theme

Once a theme has been selected, each person should proceed with the development of the idea in an individual manner. Ideas do not need to be complicated, but should be the honest expression of the individual. The ever changing shapes, colors and spaces in nature and the human-made environment can provide sources of inspiration. For example, the bark, the leaves or a knot of a tree; a typewriter may suggest letters, symbols and figures; birds may be reflected resting in a tree, in flight or even their feathers can suggest a light, airy feeling.

The artist can expand these ideas by making a sketch of those observations that are personally appealing. The drawing may have one of a number of aims — it can be a careful representation of the object as the end product; it can be a rough sketch to represent the feeling about the subject. It could also be a series of drawings exploring the subject different ways that could develop into design.

The bark of tree charcoal study is interpreted with the layering of fabrics and stitches by the author.

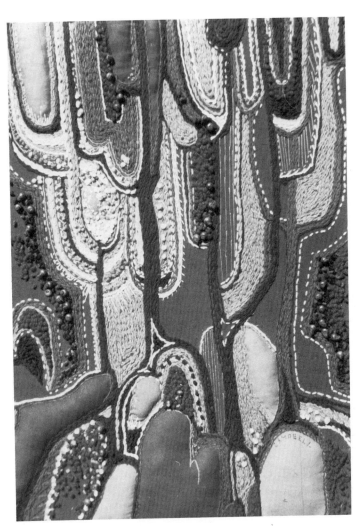

Bark of Tree. Kitty Campbell illustrates how she has interpreted the same subject. Piles of overlapping stitches, beads and trapunto produce a tactile feeling.

20

Aging dried leaves.

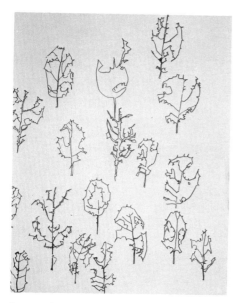

Interesting possibilities could develop from this drawing, using a variety of techniques and experimenting with different scales of working.

Clouds. Photograph by Robert Ishi.

Purely imaginative concepts derived from the natural forces of nature such as, for example, selected dried leaves could be studied for a design. The aging process has changed their shapes and can offer new inspirations to the designer.

Nature offers us limitless sources for design inspiration in all its aspects. To feel the form and movement in the mind's eye needs careful study. To catch the changing mood of the clouds, surf eroded sandstone, water flowing over boulders, can be visually exciting.

Series of drawings abstracting leaves in a design arrangement.

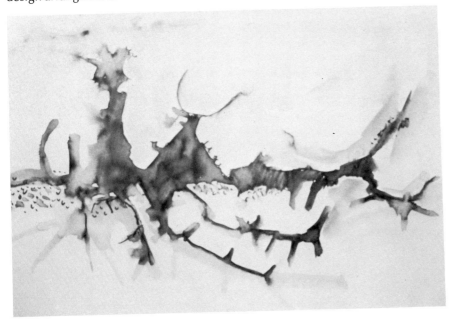

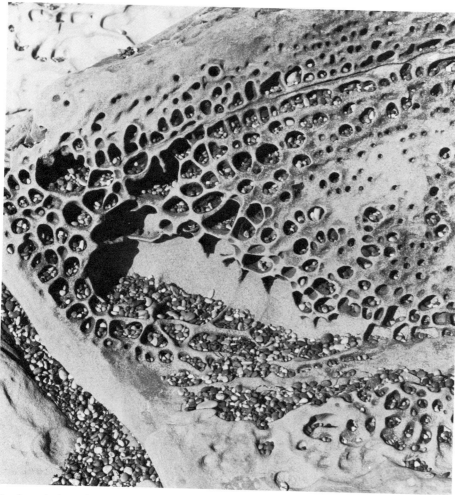

Curiosity to look inside of objects can direct ideas for shapes, lines and textures. The cross section of a cabbage can suggest fabric draped and stuffed to express the rounded wiggly shapes. The deep crevices for the fabric collage stitchery designer can be defined with running or stem stitches. The study sketch of a cross section of a pomegranate has inspired the designer, Sawaka Ashizama, to interpret the seedy interior with massed French knots.

Each person has an individual way of observing and reacting to situations and ideas. The fabric stitchery artist, like any artist/craftsperson, will visualize the medium of fabrics and threads while working on the design.

Surf eroded sandstone with pebbles and water flowing over boulders, forming rhythms and patterns. Photograph by Robert Ishi.

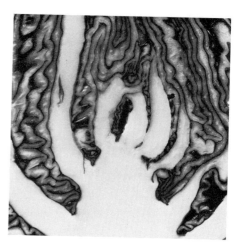

Cross section of cabbage. Photograph by Robert Ishi.

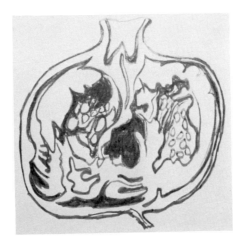

Sketch of cross section of pomegranate.

The sketch helped portray pomegranate interpreted in fabric and threads by Sawaka Ashizama.

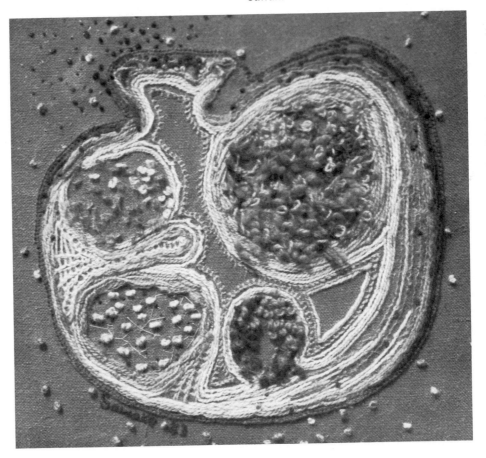

The sense of touch and feel also becomes an important part of our search for ideas. The flowers in a garden demand to be touched, as well as looked at. To appreciate the thorny, smooth or fuzzy surfaces, touching is essential.

A subject seen from different perspectives can be fascinating — such as patterns of plowed fields or mountains as seen from the air — and can inspire fabric shapes for a fabric collage stitchery. The same subject seen from an automobile or on foot can present a totally different impression.

Dandelion gone to seed makes a strong radial movement.

Layered transparent silks in blues, grays and yellows expresses the airy quality of *Bursting Seedpod* by the author. Stitched lines and pearls accent the radiating form.

Aerial view of Yosemite.

Yosemite. Joyce Oyama, inspired by the dark mountain ridges, has cut out shapes in fabric and overlapped stitches to express the rhythms and spaces.

Fabric collage stitchery by author was
inspired by the aerial view of the plowed
field and buildings.

The close inspection of objects in a landscape presents detail that can be interpreted with stitches. For instance, the magnified veining in a leaf can be created with linked chain stitches in threads of varying weights. The bubbly effect can develop into a quilted form.

Whatever the mental image, ideas must be sifted out and selected. The intuitive, skilled designer, as well as the beginner, can arrive at satisfactory results without losing the original spark of enthusiasm. The human-made environment provides a wealth of inspiration for the designer. The human-made shapes in contrast to the rhythmic natural environment, can often suggest more defined or hard-edged cut out fabric shapes.

Leaf veining. Photograph by Robert Ishi.

Overlapping fabrics and stitches by Doris Marx express the layered effect, which bears a close design relationship to the peeling effect of the Paris billboard.

Inspiration for Design Ideas

Nancy Morgan has captured the rhythmic movement of glass floats. Massed dark shadows, made with fabric, and strong vertical open rhythms, produced with chain stitches, unify the composition.

Photograph of glass floats by Nancy Morgan.

Photograph of Paris billboard.

Fire Hydrant. Sue Swanson expresses pop art. Batik, knotless netting, further embellished with French knots, and chain stitches are used, created over a styrofoam base.

Fire hydrant, a human-made form, can inspire new shapes for design.

Other Sources of Ideas for Reference

A collage sketch for a design can be made of cut up pieces of magazine illustrations and swatches of cloth glued together. Scraps of lace could illustrate how the visual textures of the lettering and linear patterns of the collage sketch might be interpreted with fabric. Parts of the collage may be developed with batik (a method of creating designs with wax, discussed in the section on techniques.)

Visits to the library, museum and special exhibitions to awaken a new awareness to current developments in related art fields can spark design ideas. For instance, a project on masks might require a study of other cultures. Characteristic materials of the culture can direct the use of fabrics, feathers, threads and dyed materials.

Gayle Stetter has employed batik, lace, handwoven strips, bones, beads and feathers in a creative mask. The burlap, dipped in glue and allowed to dry to hold the desired shape, forms the foundation.

Collage sketch can provide a source of inspiration for a design.

Cosmic Joy by Joyce Yasuhiro.

Green Landscape by Anna Ballarian.

Flower Garden by Elizabeth Adams.

Tree Bark by Kitty Campbell.

Labyrinth by Diana Brenna.

Our Mother Moist Earth by José Bénitez Sanchez.

Abandoned Joy – Bark of Tree by Anna Ballarian.

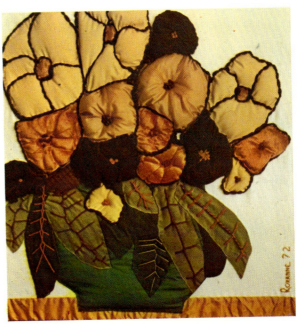

Flowers in Vase by Roxanne Clark.

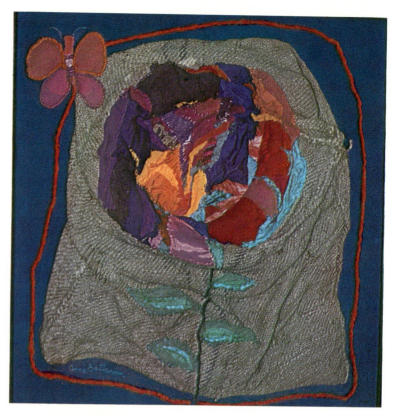

Use of Litter Bag Will Help to Keep Our Country Beautiful by Anna Ballarian.

Glass Floats by Nancy Morgan.

Fabric collage sampler with stitches by
Amy Yoshida.

My Garden Fantasy by Joanne Miller Johnson.

Peace and Joy, banner by Marilyn Brandon.

God Bless America by Anna Ballarian.

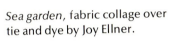
Banner by Bernalita McRostie.

Sea garden, fabric collage over
tie and dye by Joy Ellner.

Pandora's Box by Joy Ellner.

Quilted jacket by Winifred Amade.

Fabric collage pillow by Anna Ballarian.

A Bird in the Hand, a walking sleeping bag by Gayle Feller. It incorporates brilliantly colored hand-dyed velvets, cottons and batik scraps, appliquéd and stuffed against a purple background.

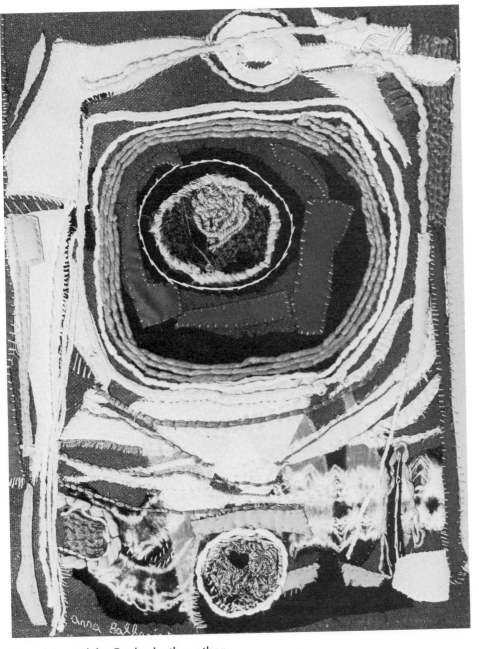

3

Methods of Developing an Original Design Idea

In and Around the Garden by the author makes use of brilliant red and green wool fabric scraps, arranged on a purple background.

Design means different things to different people. It is essentially a visual statement of the whole thought and inspiration that comes from within the artist. Designs will form according to how the artist has responded to his environment by direct experimentation with tools and materials to make a thick, thin or wiggly line or shape. Each person will find his own method of juggling lines of threads, shapes and colors of fabrics to create a desired impression with textile materials.

The Sketch

A careful sketch of a finished fabric collage stitchery can be useful to start your project. But it might be boring to make an exact representation copied from a sketch and probably lack vitality in the end product. A sketch in most cases becomes a series of trial and error decisions in recording the main lines and shapes with subtle variations of the selected theme.

The sketch does not need to be a scale drawing. It is a good idea, however, to do a preliminary sketch in proportion to the planned design. It serves as a guide and can give the artist courage to confidently cut into a fabric without fear of making a mistake. One of the first decisions is to consider whether it is to be a wall hanging, a free standing object, a body or bed covering or whatever the artist has in mind.

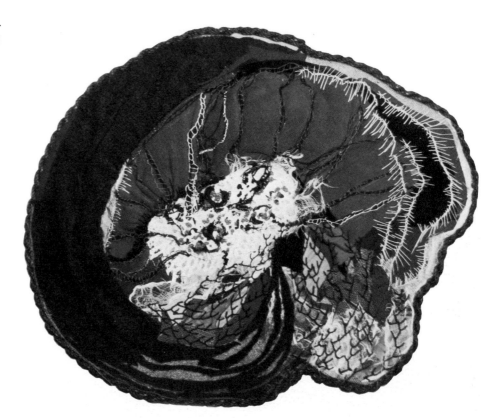

The sketch of a knot in a tree helped Diane Lee in developing her design. A free art form developed as she experimented with different textures of materials.

Along a Country Road is an interpretation of soil erosion using fabrics, laces and stitches. The result is a vitally alive idea because values were initially well established.

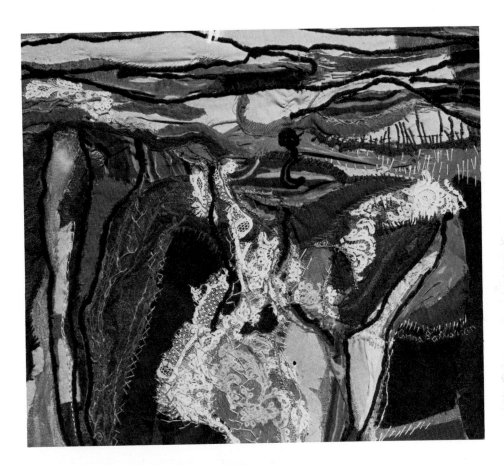

The sketch of soil erosion by author.

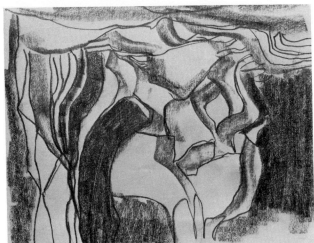

The next consideration will be the size of the project. It will influence the scale of the work. In the works of Nancy and Dewey Lipe the emphasis is on the forms in nature. Large free standing and hanging forms, often borrowed heavily from graceful jellyfish, with bright glass balls frequently interrupting the crochet and needle woven tendrils that end in bulbous fabric shapes. Satins, brocades, velvets and other lush fabrics in carefully coordinated reds, purples and blues make these large pieces. The fabrics are wrapped over metal armatures to form soft organic shapes, usually with carefully tufted cloth covering the interior and under sides of the works. Each creation invites viewer participation.

The Enchanted Chanterelle by Dewey and Nancy Lipe.

Carbuncular Womb Fleur de Viet Nam by Dewey and Nancy Lipe. Photograph by Dewey Lipe.

Methods of Developing an Original Design Idea

Experimenting Directly with Fabrics

More satisfying results can be produced by experimenting. Moving around cut-out pieces of fabric shapes, colors and lines can help achieve a pleasing design and avoid combining clashing colors. The irregular shapes from a rag bag can suggest unique ways to abstract a building, human figure or flower garden.

The way fabric textures are handled can create specific feelings. For instance, net or cheesecloth pulled apart to exposed underlying layers can represent reflections in water, smoke or deep space. The ragged frayed edge caused by pulling or tearing apart materials will produce a more expressive blending of layered effects.

Fantasy City Hall Building by Joanne Miller Johnson. Made from discarded scraps of fabrics and laces.

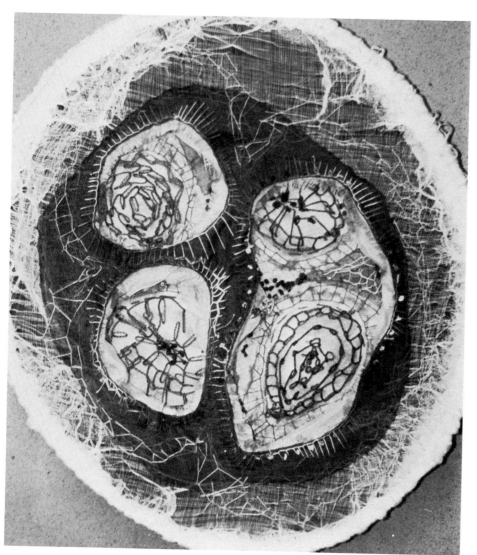

Embryo by Rosemarie Pauk is an idea observed through a microscope. Cheesecloth pulled apart, frayed, and stretched over holes produces transparent spaces.

Repeat Patterned Fabrics   Incorporating your own hand-dyed batiks and tie dyes, as well as fabrics with commercially produced repeat patterns, in your work can be a challenge.

Textural Effects for New Dimensions in Collage

Fabrics, freely draped, can produce a realistic or impressionistic feeling. For instance, a satiny fabric with its reflective quality can be pinched into ripples to express a waterfall or clouds. A piece of velour with its deep pile, when pushed into depressions can express crevices in the earth, or can be puckered for a soft animal shape, like a caterpiller.

The fabric backgrounds can be further embellished with various embroidery stitches. These, like scratches with pencil or pen, can add a new dimension to the collage. Shapes and spaces can be defined with thick and thin threads to emphasize shading in two-dimensional work.

Bob's Kites by Nancy Freeman.

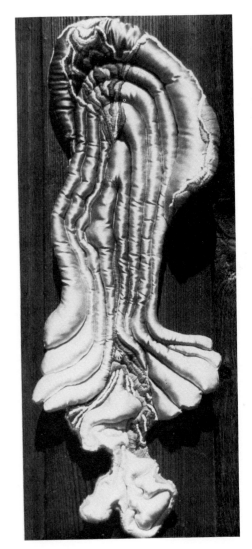

Free Form Stuffed by Nan Murphy was inspired by a waterfall. Design was drawn directly on shiny fabric and machine stitched to a background. Incisions were made in the background fabric and polyester fiber was pushed into the channeled areas. Then, colorful overcasting stitches were applied over the raised areas to further express movement of water.

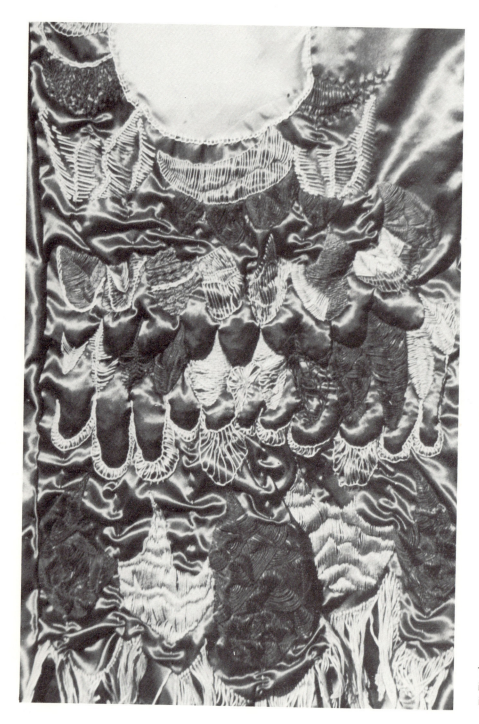

If a built-up textural effect is desired speedily, a long chain stitch can be produced with a crochet hook and incorporated into the collage. Other structured materials can be produced with threads such as knitted, lacey and knotted textures and stuck or sewn into the collage for added dimension. Original fabrics can be changed in character by pulling threads, stitching into them, darning, inserting threads, hooking or covering entire surfaces with French knots, running chain, and cross stitches. The overlapping of the various stitches can lead the eye in certain directions to define shapes and spaces within a composition.

Mass arrangements of repetitive patterns created with stuffed shapes linked together, buttons, beads, feathers and found objects, can be stitched into parts of the collage to produce unusual tactile feelings.

The natural puckering of a satiny fabric inspired the unique shapes and textures in *Wallhanging* by Elizabeth Anderson.

A Flower Garden by Annabelle Vaughan. Lightness and airiness are evoked by the use of transparent fabrics in pinks and greens. The collage was worked on the stretched fabric background.

Landscape by Tasia Smith. The strong light and dark fabrics are glued on and embellished with stitches. Long chain stitches were produced by crocheting and stitching down.

An enlarged seedpod by Janet Bellaire. Linked stuffed fabric forms and beads massed together make an emphatic appeal to touch and feel.

42

Viewing Images from Photographs

Finding a basic approach to an original design idea applies to fabric collage stitchery art, as well as in other mediums. Each person discovers a personal style of expression. It can be impressionism, realism, op-art, pop art or abstract. Art sometimes happens by accident but it often requires planning and manipulating of fabrics and threads to obtain a specific effect. Many artists maintain a file of photographs which can serve as a source for various aspects of design.

Sometimes, a portion of the photograph is visually pleasing for value contrast, line movement or unusual shapes. For instance, a landscape can be viewed upside down if the values from this view seem pleasing. A working drawing can be abstracted from the selected photograph or portion of it. From the moment the first piece of fabric is placed on a chosen background a relationship is set up between the positive (solid) shapes and the negative (surrounding) space that forms a focal interest. As lines and shapes are added to the composition, the designer should leave room to move freely in any direction. An effort should be made to simplify patterns of dark and light so the eye can easily feel the implied rhythm that the designer is trying to achieve.

Demonstration of photograph selection for sketch. Photograph by Kathie Cambiano.

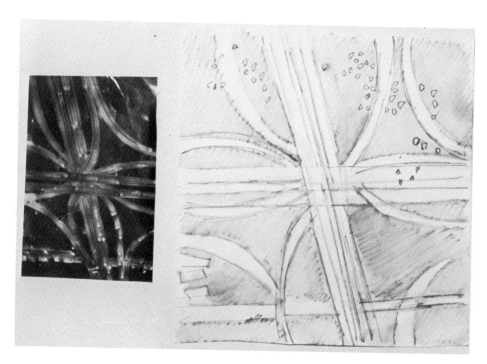

Design from a photographic swatch.

Methods of Working

In order to view the total composition easily, when moving the fabric scraps, some designers prefer to stretch the work over a rigid support. Pieces can be pinned down temporarily. Work in progress can be placed on the wall or easel to view from a distance before pieces are attached permanently.

Supporting the work on a frame helps to speed up the process when textures are produced by hooking with a rug hook or massing of French knots. Many large projects or three-dimensional forms can be supported on a table. To facilitate manipulation of fabrics for stitching or gluing, it is appropriate to keep the project loose. Sometimes loosely holding the work on the lap makes it easier to work from both sides.

Method of working on the table.

Method of sectional stuffing. Photograph by Kathie Cambiano.

Color

Color is a very personal means of expression in all visual art. At first glance it is the color that makes a strong emotional impact before one becomes aware of the form. Different feelings — love, anger, joy and excitement — can be aroused by relationship of colors. There are many theories about color. But most collage artists prefer to discover the color effects by working directly with the medium for the most satisfying results.

Color perception increases with observation. The infinite variations of color in natural forms can be a great source of inspiration. A color scheme using the values of one color can be effective. This can be seen in the subtle shade of shells, leaves, and stones or strong contrasts as seen in flowers, insects and animals. Many projects where natural forms have been used are enhanced by the selection of fabrics which express both the color and the textures of the object.

A color wheel can help one to learn what to expect when working with specific colors. Tensions and vibrations can be achieved with complementary colors. Complements are opposite on the color wheel, such as red and green, blue and orange, yellow and purple. Complements can produce a dazzling effect for an illusion of the third dimension. To subdue stronger pure colors, overlay sheer transparent, lacey fabrics. Brilliant colors will look brighter against subdued colors.

Colors are affected by surrounding colors. A shiny colored fabric will reflect light and an opaque surface will absorb light.

A dominant warm or cool scheme can unify the composition. Warm colors are reds and oranges. Cool colors are greens and blues.

One of the hardest decisions is to know when to stop. The excitement of the project and physical involvement makes one reluctant to bring the work to an end. But a sensitive designer is aware of the proportion of the line, form, shape, texture and color. Look at the work from a distance as well as close up to aid in making your decision.

4

Organization

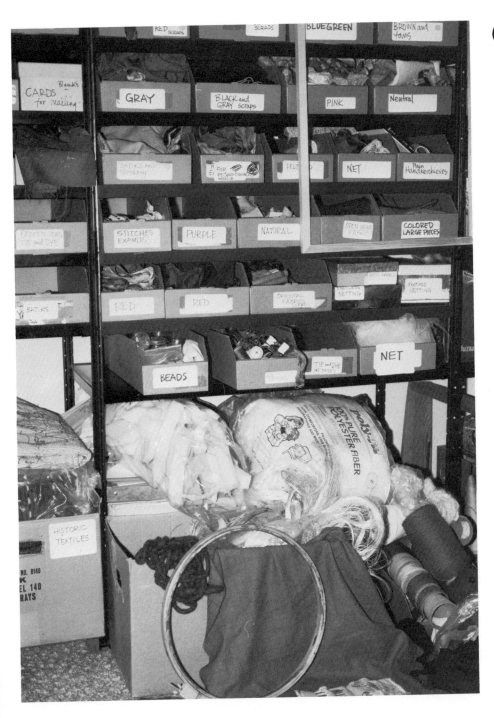

This storage system illustrates a possible method of cataloging materials.

Equipment Needed for Fabric Collage

1. A sharp pair of scissors
2. Straight pins
3. needles
      tapestry long eye
      crewel
      round eye
4. Adhesives
      Sobo glue
      Pellon or Stitch Witchery
      liquid cloth
      spee-dee fabric and
      canvas cement
5. dyes (see further details)
6. sewing and embroidery yarns
7. iron and ironing board
8. sketch book and drawing paper
9. pencils or pens
10. sewing machine
11. stretcher bars

Adhesives

For the collage artist gluing can serve two purposes. It can become a permanent hold or it can be used instead of pins to freely experiment with pieces before attaching them to the background. When there are many small pieces which are massed together to form a larger shape, it might also be advisable to hold the unit together with glue. Fusible webs such as Pellon or Stitch Witchery are a neat way of holding fabric to fabric. It is washable and dry cleanable. The fusible web is cut to the needed shape, placed between layers of fabric to be fused, covered with wet press cloth and steam set to fuse.

Firm pressing for ten minutes will adhere fabrics together.

Sobo, a more versatile glue, offers greater freedom for experimentation because it stays tacky long enough to move fabric pieces around. It is water soluble, dries clear and is a strong flexible bond. Sobo would be safer to use, especially with children, and is an efficient way of attaching large areas of fabric.

If one is searching for a quick, easy hold for very heavy materials, such as carpet or upholstery scraps, a glue called liquid cloth will do the job. This glue dries clear and is washable, but has some disadvantages. It is volatile, it must be used in a well ventilated area and should be applied sparingly on thin and knitted fabrics. It cannot be used on acetates.

Work Space

The fabric collage stitchery artist must have suitable work space. It is essential to have a wall space and large work table. For better perspective, tack the work to the wall. Water and clothesline should be accessible for freedom to dye materials when special effects are desired. An iron, ironing board and sewing machine should be easily available so work can progress comfortably without unnecessary physical inconvenience.

Storage

A well organized storage space aids in selecting the wide range of colors and textures in fabrics needed for a satisfactory working palette. A corner of the kitchen, basement or garage can be reserved for the cataloguing of fabrics, threads and other needed miscellaneous supplies. Each person soon works out a system suited to one's needs.

For quick identification, polythene transparent bags are an efficient storage container. Baskets or boxes may be tipped on their sides and stacked for easy access of materials.

Needles, pins and other tools.

Adhesives. Photograph by Kathie Cambiano.

Collecting a Fabric Palette

A plentiful supply of a wide selection of fabric scraps in a variety of colors, patterns and textures can add excitement to creating a fabric collage stitchery. Imported fabrics of every description and many brilliantly colored fabrics of unusual design can be purchased in department stores and local yardage shops. Remnants can be found at bargain prices to start your collection. Once your fascination to create with fabrics is known, friends will shower you with fabric ends. The odd irregular shapes from a seamstress' scraps can be priceless. Decorators' outdated sample books can also be a fabric source. The concern today for ecology makes one aware of imaginative use of these discards.

Visiting flea markets, Salvation Army, Goodwill or thrift shops, where mill ends from factories, spoiled rolls of fabrics and miscellaneous objects such as beads, sequins, cords, ribbons, laces, fur and metal scraps can be found, is a good start to building your collection. Add these to your collection even though you are not sure at the moment of how you will use them. A scrap of gold braid might provide the finishing touch.

Other found objects such as shells, bones, pebbles with holes and broken mirrors can be worth collecting. Soup bones, chicken and fish bones, bleached and sawed off in various thicknesses, can add the dimension needed for a dramatic effect. A collection of transparent materials, such as nylon net, sheer organdie and old nylon stockings, can serve to obtain subtle gradations of color, similar to those in a watercolor painting. Cheese cloth is invitingly cheap and easy to get. Dyes for specific colors are also needed. To further enrich your fabric palette, collect old lace curtains, discarded sheer knitted clothes, crocheted pieces, needle laces and silk from old neckties.

Romantic Fan Fantasy by Helen Kastohryz illustrates how a decorator's sample swatches can provide an inspiration for design.

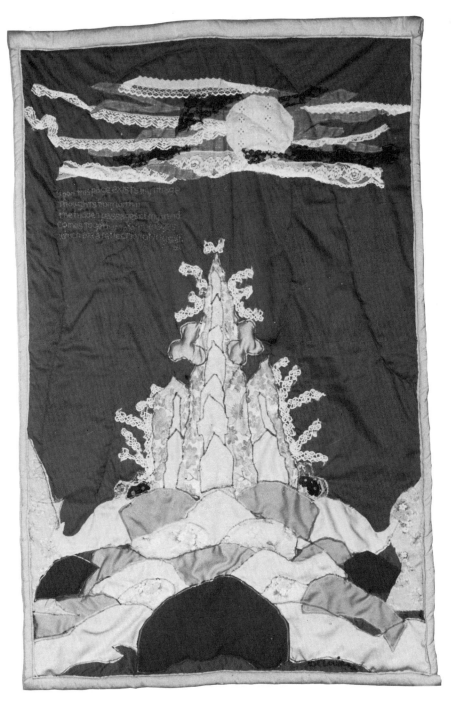

Reflected Images of Myself. Dorothy Louie has made use of lace scraps to create textural effects.

50

Three dimensional *Red Rose* by Beverly
McKinzie. A blue gray quilted
background strongly sets off the velour
and satin.

Artist Jean Varda, noted for his colorful fabric collage, created imaginative designs with mostly scraps from discarded old clothing. "With small pieces of cotton and silks, scissors and glue and dash of paint, he dressed his women in irradiations; his colors breathed like flesh and the fine spun lines pulsated like nerves."[1]

Choice of Background

There is no rule that one must begin with a special kind of background material. It can be heavy, thin, loose or compact. It depends upon the direction one takes as the design develops. Experimenting with the fabric scraps may reveal a need for a particular color or texture to set them off. Several pieces of cloth of different qualities could be connected to express a feeling. Often the background fabric for a project is chosen first and can get one off to a happy start. Felt is a sturdy ground, if creating a hard smooth edge is desired, because it is easy to manipulate. Linen, burlap, and loosely woven decorators' materials can serve as backgrounds for stage settings, window displays, clothing or other environmental collage. Wool salvaged from old blankets or clothing can provide firm backgrounds for a picture or banner.

[1]*Collages* by Anais Nin (about Jean Varda)

Blue Queen, fabric collage by Jean Varda. Courtesy of the Monterey Art Museum.

Scrap Hat by Lucille Margosian is a sensitive handling of discarded neckties in a collage.

Threads and Yarns

A collection of a wide selection of threads and yarns should be kept on hand to encourage experimental work. Almost anything in the way of threads and yarns can be utilized. Embroidery flosses in all colors and textures are especially good if work is to be laundered very often.

Needles

Basically, three types of needles will serve most of your needs. Select needles which allow the threads to pass through the eye of the needle without too much of a struggle. A *tapestry needle* with a long eye and blunt end is useful for heavy threads and loosely woven fabrics. *Crewel needles* are used with thinner threads and are pointed for use on finer materials. For making French knots and bullion knots, a *round-eyed needle* is required so that knots can slip off the needle easily. Just as an artist selects his drawing tools, the fabric collage artist will need to experiment with many needles to find what feels right in one's hand and easily pierces through the cloth being used.

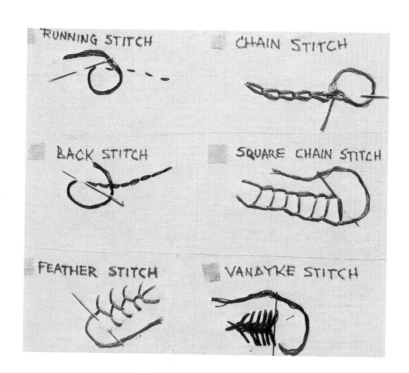

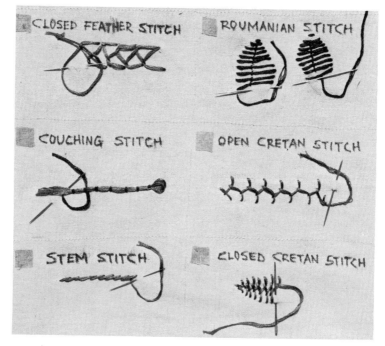

Basic Stitches

The imaginative use of stitches for decorative effects becomes an important part of fabric collage. Therefore, a knowledge of stitches is useful for the fabric collage artist. Basic stitches, shown here, are running, back, couching, chain and French knots. These are all one needs to know to get started.

Dyes

Do not depend entirely on dye colors right out of the package. Mix your own color in order to achieve an original color. Quality dyes such as Cushing, Putnam, Althouse, Procion and Fibrec are available and easy to use. Should more subtle colors be desired, and if one has the time to experiment, vegetable dyeing may prove to be a solution. For example, onion skins yield a rich golden brown, chrysanthemums produce a bright yellow. Experiments with plants from your own garden can provide unusual colors.

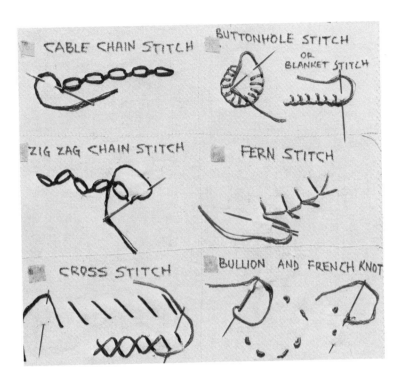

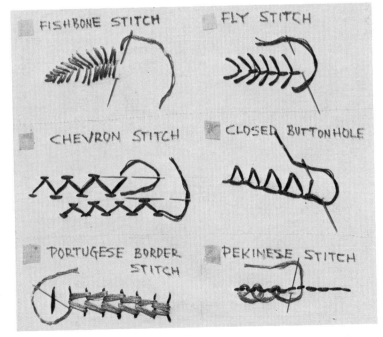

Hallelujah by Debbie Hart. Colored felt, hand-stitched appliqué. Sequins and stitches add sparkle. Trapunto in the vertical white areas makes an appealing tactile quality.

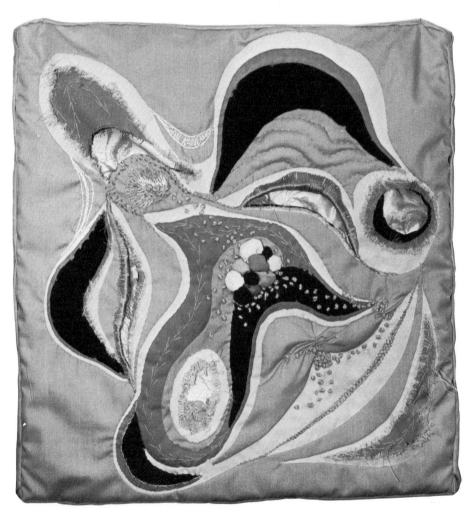

5
Techniques That May Lead to New Directions

Reverse appliqué with stitchery to show imaginative directions of this technique by Gail Kanemoto.

Mariska Karasz, the forerunner of adventuring with stitches, made a complete break from the more formal counting of threads. She created dramatic effects by elongating and loosening tension. She crossed some stitches over and under each other and worked them into different fabric backgrounds. Her influence has led collage artists to enrich surfaces with ribbons, bones, beads, scraps of fur and piles of stitches. A study of the work of contemporary fabric artists will reveal that Karasz and other early artists have had an influence on the techniques now used.

Colonial women designed beautiful quilts using pieces of hand-dyed materials. These quilts have served as inspiration for other artists who use their own batik scraps to create impressive designed wall hangings and quilts that are built up with stuffed forms projecting from them.

Some people produce a mosaic-like quality achieved with technical expertise. French knots, and long running stitches for textural effects are subtly used to accent parts of the composition. The illustrated examples show various combinations of techniques used to produce unusual art objects to ornament the body, to decorate a wall or davenport, to cover the bed, stand free on a table or on the floor.

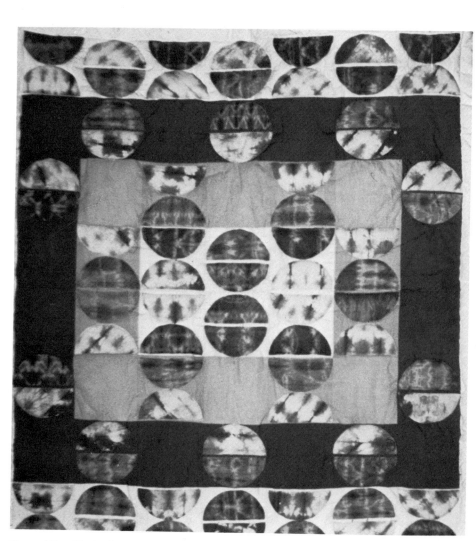

Tie and Dye Circles by Janet Bellaire illustrates the use of her own hand-dyed materials.

Appliqué is sewing or gluing pieces of cloth on top of each other or embroidered together. The effect of a raised design results as each layer of fabric is stitched or glued down working from the bottom to the top.

Reverse Appliqué is stacking layers of cloth of contrasting colors. Principal shapes of the design are cut out. Then smaller elements are cut from the next layer, and the process is repeated. The edges of each layer usually are carefully turned under so that no raw edges will show. Today, ravelled, raw edges are acceptable. Edges can be secured by overcasting stitches or gluing.

Reverse appliqué showing layered effect. Rose Burke.

Patchwork skirt by Linda Witt. Makes use of varied textures of fabric, sensitively arranged and multistitched over a muslin foundation.

Quilting is two layers of material joined together with an interlayer of padding. Years ago the primary purpose of filler was for warmth. Today modern materials such as polyester fiber and polyfoam provide warmth, but are light weight, easy to care for and easy to sew. Quilting is popular for bed cover, wearing apparel and banners. The technique is also used for creating low relief designs in three-dimensional forms. The bottom layer is usually muslin or any sturdy fabric. Designs vary from randomly selected fabric patches to carefully planned ideas forming the top layer.

Trapunto is padding sections of the appliqué design to produce high relief. Cotton batting, rags, bits of yarn, polyester fiber or polyfoam is stuffed under the surface of design areas as work progresses. The stuffing can be built up through an incision made behind the design that has already been stitched down.

Geometric Quilt by Celia Clark is in orange, yellow and black. Inspired by experimenting with ideas on squared paper.

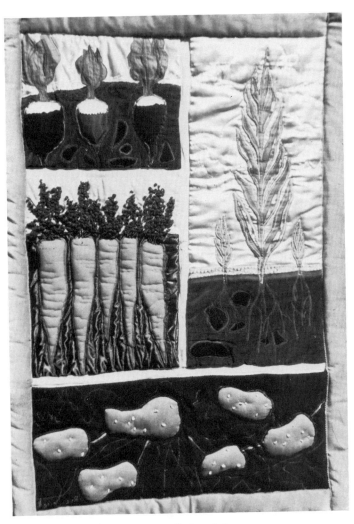

Simulated Rectangles by Karen Robbins. Black bias tape defines the strong line to produce the feeling of a leaded stained glass window.

Vegetable Garden by Ruth Lovell. Careful observation of her subject has inspired the artist to make imaginative use of stitches, appliqué and trapunto in building up vegetable forms.

60

Jewelled Quilt by Diane Centers. Inspired by her watercolor painting. The top is joined to the fill and the bottom by means of one color of yarn pulled through at regular intervals and knotted on top.

Wings by Anne Sprague. Design was machine stitched over a background fabric. Small areas were stuffed through incisions made through the back. Free crochet stitches were applied to depressed areas to define feather-like shapes.

Flower Garden by Joy Ellner is an invitation to touch and feel the shiny, raised leatherette flower forms.

The Square Quilt by Lorri Basque. Top layer was put together by machine stitching from the wrong side. Filler was sandwiched in between top and bottom layers by machine stitching, with bottom layer brought to the front to form the border.

Twelve black and white portraits by author. Various textured black and white fabrics are built up in sections for modeled effects.

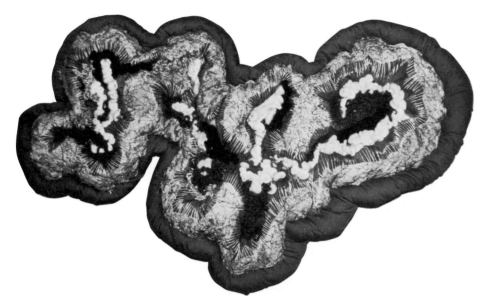

Seaweed by Gayle Stetter. A stuffed freeform shape in stitched fabric collage.

To express a theme, *Beach Pebbles* by Diane Fuller. Trapunto technique is used to make rounded shapes. Running, feather, and French knot stitches create the seaweed overlapping the pebble forms.

The Medicine Cabinet by Sally Emeson represents a series of three-dimensional tactile forms that invites viewer participation.

Orange Crate by Ruth Lovell is expressive of pop art.

Travel Bag by Maggie Brosnan. A soft sculpture in brilliant shades of red. Stitched collage of hand-dyed scraps of velvet form the body of the bag, with fur lining that invites the viewer to feel inside.

Mixed media in painting or sculpture shows that many artists, other than fiber artists, are employing stitching on fabrics. Fabric collage stitchery can also combine many techniques: appliqué, stitching, weaving, hooking, knotless netting, batik, tie and dye and other fabric treatments. Three-dimensional forms and pillows are popular ideas for fabric collage stitchery. The pillow as a design problem provides great scope to experiment with a stuffed, three-dimensional form.

Banners are widely recognized as an art expression, especially in recent times. They provide an exciting graphic means to add surface richness and symbolic meaning in contemporary homes, churchs and other public buildings.

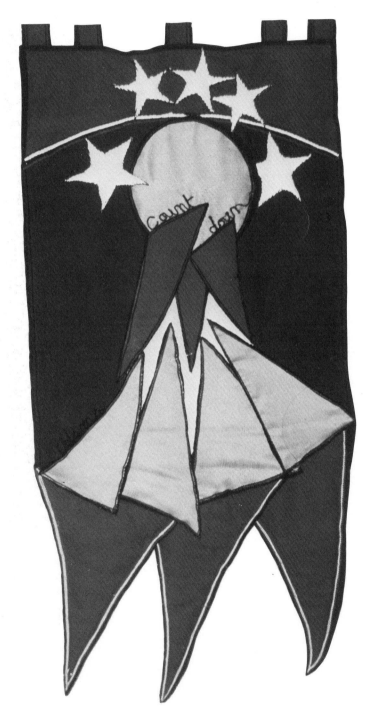

Count Down by Elizabeth Adams is fabric appliquéd by sewing machine. Lettering is embroidered.

66

Fred Flutterby by Lisa Horn.

Stuffed Seedpod by Judie Dinwiddie. A radiating tie and dye, pinched into a central depressed area, is accented with chain stitch and French knots. The appliqué velvet sheath-like form, outlined with the blanket stitch, gently rolls inward to emphasize the space.

Cranberry by Susie Schwoob. A study of the cross section of a cranberry, interpreted with red and white satin. The seed forms are stuffed and heavily textured with French knots, creating an inviting contrast.

Waiting at the Airport by the author. It combines batik, appliqué and piles of stitches. The legs and head of this turtle are stuffed with polyester fiber and attached to the stuffed body of the animal.

Me and My Father by Shirley Evans. A quilted banner using hobbies as the theme. A well defined figure on the bicycle is created with massed stitches.

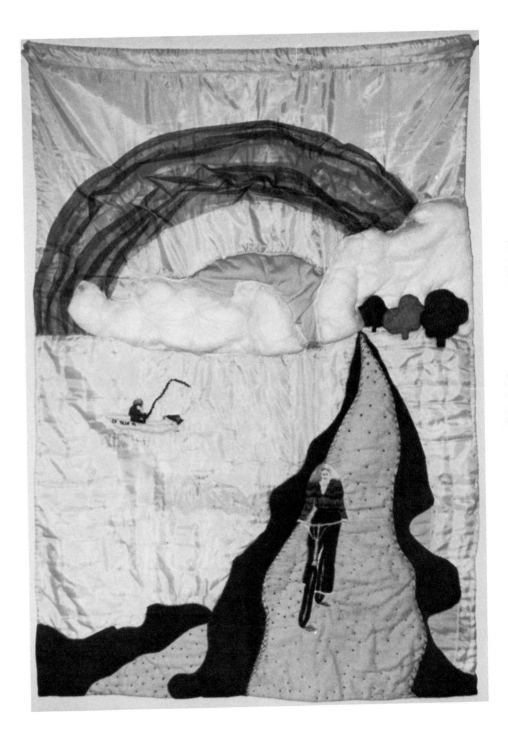

Local Hangout by Gayle Ash is a simple horizontal composition appliquéd against a dark blue background. Cross stitched stars hold the three layers of this quilted banner together.

A Victorian Building by Joanne Miller Johnson. A pleasing subject for a composition of a variety of forms and textures inspired by the building's shape. Dyed laces were employed to illustrate the architectural textures. The sky is created with tie and dye fabric.

Batik scraps embellished with French knots by author.

Larry Bergher has produced a sun symbol with tie and dye, into which he has appliquéd and stitched radiating lines. The form is padded, hand stitched and framed.

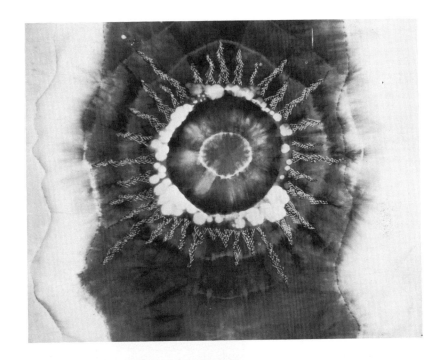

Explosion by Diane Di Salvo. Tie and dye inspired the direction of the design. Massed, straight machine stitching expresses the freeform shape and the long hand stitches create emphatic movement.

Outer Space by the author. The circular areas were cut out. The open holes were gathered up, tied and dyed. Then the entire piece was appliquéd on a light background. The cut out pieces were separately tied and dyed, then appliquéd back into the wall hanging. Hand, as well as machine, stitching is used.

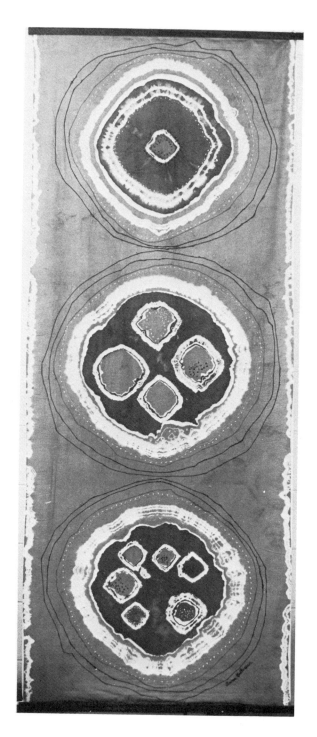

6

Presenting the Finished Product

Early Morning, Oh How Wonderful by the author. Strong radiating lines of fabric, machine stitched to stand on edge, interpret the mushroom coral. This work illustrates a method of framing a fabric collage.

The method of presenting the work in the home, public building or in an exhibition will be determined by its function. The importance of fine execution of the technique on outstanding design should never be underestimated, but a fine piece of work can be ruined by a careless presentation. The frame, armature or pedestal used is often of vital importance in the success of the finished piece.

If the completed art work does not drape to your satisfaction, proper pressing can improve it. A method of pressing is to wrinkle two sheets of brown wrapping paper, approximately 12″ x 18″, until they are soft like cloth. Wet them. Place one wet piece under and one over the area to be pressed. Hold the dry, hot iron over the top of the work and gradually steam dry the parts to be smoothed. The starch in the paper gives the fabric body which allows it to drape nicely. Handle the iron so that areas of the design to be high or low relief are not damaged by overly aggressive pressing. Constant handling of a piece while working on it may cause irregularity in the shape. In order to correct this measure, pin the work on a padded table and steam iron as suggested above.

Most fabric collage artists generally prefer to mount their own creations. Work can be framed, draped or free standing, depending upon the shape and size. The finished piece can be stretched over stretcher bars, brought around to the back and stapled. No frame is necessary. If framing is desired, a simple frame is often best. If the design consists of raised forms, the work should be mounted to come forward rather than recessed. Wood stain or acrylic paint, mixed to a color that will complement the fabric and stitches, can be rubbed into a natural wood frame.

Draping can become an essential element in the overall design. Whether it is to have a particular finish, such as a fringe, tassels, loops or a rolled stuffed irregular border must be carefully considered. The support at the top of a banner or quilt can be a dowel rod, metal rod or a branch. Lead drapery weights can be stitched and concealed in the bottom of the hanging to keep it taut.

An awareness of what has been done in the past should be kept in mind while attending contemporary exhibitions. To observe how artists are presenting works of art will help make one aware of effective ways to display fabric collage stitcheries.

Christmas ornament by Marilyn Bauriedel. Rolling edges produce irregular draping.

Los Palomas by Nancy Freeman. Realistic design imaginatively abstracted. Materials of many textures machine stitched with zig-zag stitch.

Scrap pillow illustrates that fabric collage stitchery as an art can be presented in the form of a pillow.

Cube Inside of Plastic Box by Laurie Brown illustrates a method of presentation for a three-dimensional work.

Suggested Bibliography

Books

Belfer, Nancy, *Designing in Stitching and Applique*, Worcester, Mass.: Davis Publications, Inc., 1972.

Designing in Batik and Tie Dye, Worcester, Mass.: Davis Publications, Inc., 1972.

Colby, Averil, *Quilting*, London and New York: B. T. Batsford, Ltd., and Scribner, 1971.

Concepts of Design Series, Worcester, Mass.: Davis Publications, Inc.
Part I – Elements (1974).
Brommer, Gerald F., *Space*
Gatto, Joseph A., *Color and Value*
Horn, George F., *Texture*
Porter, Albert W., *Shape and Form*
Selleck, Jack, *Line*

Part II – Principles (1975).
Bommer, Gerald F., *Movement and Rhythm*
Gatto, Joseph A., *Emphasis*
Horn, George F., *Balance and Unity*
Porter, Albert W., *Pattern*
Selleck, Jack, *Contrast*

D'Harcourt, Raoul, *Textiles of Ancient Peru and Their Techniques*, Seattle: University of Washington Press, 1962.

de Saumarez, Maurice, *Basic Design: The Dynamics of Visual Form*, London: Studio Vista, 1964.

Evans, Helen, *Man the Designer*, New York: Macmillan, 1973.

Frew, Hannah, *Three Dimensional Embroidery*, New York: Van Nostrand Reinhold, 1975.

Furst, Peter T. *Myth in Art: a Huichol Depicts His Reality*, Los Angeles: Latin American Center, University of California at Los Angeles, 1973.

Gray, Jennifer, *Machine Embroidery: Technique and Design*, New York: Van Nostrand Reinhold, 1973.

Guild, Vera P., *Painting with Stitches*, Worcester, Mass.: Davis Publications, Inc., 1976.

Guyler, Vivian Varney, *Design in Nature*, Worcester, Mass.: Davis Publications, Inc., 1970.

Howell-Koehler, Nancy, *Soft Jewelry: Design, Techniques, Materials*, Worcester, Mass.: Davis Publications, Inc., 1976.

Hutton, Helen, *The Techniques of Collage*, New York: Watson-Guptill Publications, 1968.

Johnston, Meda Parker and Kaufman, Glen, *Design on Fabrics*, New York: Van Nostrand Reinhold, 1967.

Jones, Mary Eirwen, *A History of Western Embroidery*, New York: Watson-Guptill Publications, 1969.

Kay, Frances, *Starting Fabric Collage*, London and New York: Studio Vista, Ltd. and Watson-Guptill Publications, 1969.

Krevitsky, Nik, *Stitchery: Art and Craft*, New York: Van Nostrand Reinhold, 1973.

Laliberte, Norman and McIlhany, Sterling, *Banners and Hangings*, New York: Van Nostrand Reinhold, 1966.

Laury, Jean and Aiken, Joyce, *Creating Body Coverings*, New York: Van Nostrand Reinhold, 1974.

Lesch, Alma, *Vegetable Dyeing*, New York: Watson-Guptill Publications, 1970.

Lumholtz, Carl, *Unknown Mexico*, Glorieta, New Mexico: The Rio Grande Press, Vol. II, 1973.

Maile, Anne, *Tie and Dye as a Present Day Craft*, London and New York: Mills and Boon, Ltd. and Taplinger Publishing Co., 1969.

Malcolm, Dorothea C., *Design: Elements and Principles*, Worcester, Mass.: Davis Publications, Inc., 1972.

Meilach, Dona, *Contemporary Batik and Tie Dye*, New York: Crown Publishing Co., 1972.

Negrin, Juan, *The Huichol Creation of the World*, Yarn Tablas by Jose Benitez Sanches and Tulukila Carrillo, E. B. Crocker Gallery and San Jose Art Museum, 1975.

Rainey, Sarita R., *Wall Hangings: Designing with Fabric and Thread*, Worcester, Mass.: Davis Publications, Inc., 1971.

Weaving Without a Loom, Worcester, Mass.: Davis Publications, Inc., 1966.

Seitz, William C., *The Art of Assemblage*, New York: The Museum of Modern Art, 1968.

Short, Erian, *Embroidery and Fabric Collage*, London and New York: Pitman and Scribner, 1973.

Sjodin, Kerstin, *Ideas in Textiles and Threads*, New York: Van Nostrand Reinhold, 1973.

Strache, Wolfe, *Forms and Patterns in Nature*, New York: Pantheon, 1973.

Timmons, Virginia Gayheart, *Art Materials, Techniques, Ideas*, Worcester, Mass.: Davis Publications, Inc., 1974.

Periodicals

American Fabrics, Doric Publishing Co., Inc., 24 East 38th Street, New York 10016

Art Week, weekly newspaper, P.O. Box 2496, Castro Valley, Calif. 94546

Craft Horizons, American Crafts Council, 44 West 53rd Street, New York 10019

Crafts, Crafts Advisory Committee, 12 Waterloo Place, London SWY 4 AU

Embroidery, The Embroiders' Guild, 73 Wimpole Street, London WIM 8 AX

Arts and Crafts Books Dealers

Book Barn, P.O. Box 256, Avon, Connecticut 06001

Textile Book Service, 1447 East 2nd Street, P.O. Box 907, Plainfield, New Jersey 07060

Unicorn (Craft and Hobby Book Service), 5525 Wilkins Court, Rockville, Maryland 20852

Source of Supplies

Adhesives

Sobo Glue
Liquid Glue
Spee-dee
Fusible webs, Pellon, Easy
Shaper or Stitch Witchery

Yardage shops and
department store
notions departments

Stuffing Materials

Polyester fill
Dacron fill
Cotton batting

Department store,
yardage and fabric
shops

Storage Boxes

Fidelity Products Co.
7051 Pennsylvania Avenue South
Minneapolis, Minnesota 55426

Tharco Sales Company
P.O. Box 2355
265 Hegenberger Road
Oakland, California 94614

Some Suggested Suppliers for Special Items

Dharma Trading Company
1604 4th Street
San Rafael, California 94902

Yarns, Procion, Cushing Dyes

Dick Blick
P.O. Box 1267
Galesburg, Illinois 61401

General craft equipment

Fibrec Incorporated
2815 18th Street
San Francisco, California 94110

Reactive dyes

Folklorico
442 Ramona
Palo Alto, California

Yarns, beads, books

Lamb's End
165 West 9 Mile
Ferndale, Michigan 48220

Feathers, yarns, stuffing, beads

Straw into Gold
5509 College Street
Oakland, California 94618

Natural dyes, scales

Testfabrics Incorporated
55 Vandam Street
New York, New York 10013

Fabrics for dyeing

Yarn Depot
545 Sutter Street
San Francisco, California 94102

Yarns and books

Althouse Dyes:
Althouse Chemical Division
Crompton and Knowles Corporation
Reading, Pennsylvania 19603

Check the yellow pages of your local telephone directory under the headings: fabrics, yardage, yarns, threads, beads, feathers, leather, dyes, weaving, polyfoam, art supplies.

Fabric collage pillow by the author.

80

Acknowledgements

I would like to thank the many persons who have helped make this book possible, especially my students who have encouraged the writing of this book. Fabric collage stitchery artists and students have generously contributed photographs and been helpful in allowing me to photograph their work. They are all credited by caption.

I am most appreciative of the constant encouragement of my friend and colleague, Dr. Helen Evans, author and teacher of design.

Gayle Feller, arts and crafts teacher and a former student, who has assisted me generously. She has read the manuscript, typed it, and made valuable suggestions. I am most grateful for her patience and audience.

I am indebted to the editors of Davis Publications for editing the material and encouraging me to carry on with this project.

All photographs are taken by the author unless otherwise credited.

Still Life by Nancy Freeman. Sewing machine appliqué. The use of commercially patterned fabrics is imaginatively handled.